M000116146

Marine Life For Young Readers

# Coral

## Contents

Text by Stanley L. Swartz
Photography by Robert Yin

DOMINIE PRESS
Pearson Learning Group

## About Corals

Corals look like plants. But corals are **animals**. Corals live in the water. They cannot live in the air.

◄ Star Coral

Corals come in many shapes. They have a hard body. It is called a **skeleton**. The coral on the beach is a skeleton.

◀ **Mushroom Coral**

## Soft Corals

Some corals are soft. They feel like jelly. Sea fans are soft corals. They live on **coral reefs**.

◀ Gorgonian Sea Fan

## Hard Corals

Some corals are **hard**. They feel like rocks. Bubble corals are hard corals. They live on coral reefs, too.

◀ Bubble Hard Coral

Hard coral can be sharp. Ships can sink when they hit reefs. Sharp coral can hurt divers. Some corals are **poisonous**.

◀ **Acropora Coral**

## Coral Reefs

Coral **gardens** are called reefs. Coral reefs live in warm water. Coral likes moving water. Water brings food to the coral.

◄ Coral Reef

There are three main types of coral reefs. One is a **fringing reef**. Fringing reefs are hooked to land. Many different corals live on this type of reef.

◀ Coral Reef

The second type of reef is a **barrier reef**. There is water between the barrier reef and land. Barrier reefs are very large. One barrier reef is more than a thousand miles long.

◄ Soft Coral

The third type of reef is an atoll. An atoll is shaped like a **ring**. There is water in the ring. People live on some big atolls.

◀ **Pink Soft Coral**

There are many colors in coral reefs. Red coral is **expensive**. It is cut and polished. It is used to make rings and necklaces.

◀ Soft Coral

Coral reefs are made up of living animals. They can be **damaged**. Boats and divers can harm them. We should protect coral reefs.

◄ **Gorgonian Sea Fan**

# Glossary

| | |
|---|---|
| **animals:** | Living organisms, not plants |
| **barrier reef:** | A long, narrow reef that is separated from land |
| **coral reefs:** | Hard shelves of coral |
| **damaged:** | Harmed or hurt |
| **expensive:** | Something that costs a lot of money |
| **fringing reef:** | A coral reef close to land |
| **gardens:** | Collections of living things |
| **hard:** | Firm, not soft |
| **poisonous:** | Something that can make you ill or kill you |
| **ring:** | Something that forms a circle |
| **skeleton:** | The frame of bones supporting an animal's body |

# Index